tea cup reading

SASHA FENTON

SEVEN DIALS

This edition first published in Great Britain in 2019 by Seven Dials,
an imprint of the Orion Publishing Group Ltd
Carmelite House, 50 Victoria Embankment,
London, EC4Y 0DZ
An Hachette UK Company

Previously published in the US in 2002 as *Tea Cup Reading:
The Ancient Art of Tasseography*, by Weiser Books, an imprint of
Red Wheel/Weiser, LLC © 2002 by Sasha Fenton

1 3 5 7 9 10 8 6 4 2

Interior design by Kathryn Sky-Peck
Illustrations © Sasha Fenton

DISCLAIMER

*The information in this book is not in any way a substitute for receiving conventional
medical treatment or consulting a physician. All the practices in this book are to be
used as an addition to existing treatments to assist the healing process and should be
fully explored only in conjunction with suitable training. Neither the author nor the
publisher assumes any liability at all for any damage caused through the application
or misapplication of procedures and statements contained in this book.*

A CIP catalogue record for this book
is available from the British Library.

ISBN: 9781409170334
eISBN: 9781409170341

Printed and bound by CPI Group (UK), Ltd, Croydon, CR0 4YY

www.orionbooks.co.uk

Contents

Part One: About Tea and Coffee

Part One: Reading the Cup

Part One

ABOUT
TEA AND
COFFEE

Tasseography

1

Anybody can read tea leaves and coffee grounds, because all it takes is the ability to see shapes made by tea and coffee leavings. My book shows you how to go about it and it contains a dictionary of symbols for interpretation purposes.

Tea leaf reading was once very popular in Britain, Ireland and the countries that were settled by Irish and British people. It has gone out of fashion in latter years, partly due to the invention of the teabag, but probably much more due to the invention of the television, which brought an end to so many home-based pastimes. Once upon a time, everyone had an aunt or grandma who read the leaves and the skill was passed down from one generation to the next. Anyone who had a touch of psychic ability learned to give readings to their friends and relatives and this ability was so prevalent that it remained an amateur skill rather than a professional matter. This form of reading is not difficult and it doesn't depend upon special calculations or even basic literacy, so cup reading has always been open to anyone who wanted to learn it.

Coffee-ground reading is practically unheard of in the UK or Ireland but it is well known in the Middle East, Mediterranean countries, Latin America and in countries to which Latin or Middle Eastern people gravitated. Coffee-ground reading is still going strong in less developed and industrialized countries and it still works very well, so there is no reason why you shouldn't learn to do it for yourself.

The fancy name for this kind of reading is tasseography. This comes from the French tasse meaning cup and the ancient Greek root graphos, which relates to writing or drawing. Therefore, tasseography means being able to read the pictures that form in a cup.

If you are interested in the dramatically fascinating story of how the cultivation and sale of tea and coffee spread around the world, take a look at the next two short chapters that outline the history of these heartwarming beverages.

The History
of Tea

2

The tea plant is native to China and it has been known there for around 5,000 years but it took a windy day and a hygiene-conscious Emperor to bring the drink into existence. Legend tells us that tea as a drink was accidentally discovered in 2737 B.C. by a Chinese Emperor called Shen Nong. This was said to have occurred when some tea leaves accidentally fell into a pot of boiling water. It is known that Shen Nong was interested in science and hygiene and that it was he who determined that drinking water should be boiled as a safety precaution. When the Emperor tried the boiled water with the tea leaves infused in it, he realized that he had discovered a refreshing new drink.

A Buddhist monk called Lu Yu wrote the first book on tea, and it was he who defined the different types of tea cultivation and preparation. In addition to its more prosaic form as a drink, Chinese tea preparation took on a mystical form. It was this strange practice that eventually transferred itself to Japan and developed into the famous Japanese tea ceremony.

Tea-leaf reading certainly originated in China and it spread throughout neighboring countries as each in turn took up the cultivation of tea.

The first traders to bring tea to Europe were the Portuguese. They carried cargoes of tea to Lisbon and from there the tea-drinking habit spread to France, Holland and the Baltic countries. The Dutch became confirmed tea-drinkers and it was the export of tea that helped to found Holland as a major trading country. Only when England settled down after the Civil War and was able to concentrate once again on overseas trade did tea start to arrive in the British Isles, this being around 1653. The price was kept artificially high, which meant that only the wealthy and privileged classes could afford to buy tea, but by 1708 tea began to come into the country in sufficient quantities and at a price that made it accessible to ordinary people.

The Chinese wisely tried to keep the secrets of tea-growing to themselves in order to maintain their monopoly on the trade. However, a Scottish botanist called Robert Fortune who actually spoke Mandarin was able to sneak into China and with the help of a Chinese friend, he managed to take some seeds away with him. The tea seeds reached India where many crops were grown, lost, improved upon, lost and grown again until the techniques became properly understood. The increasing size of the crops from the subcontinent brought the prices down and the incredibly fast clipper ships brought cargoes to Britain at great speed. The price came tumbling down and the populations of Britain and Ireland as a whole took to tea drinking in a major way.

Until the late 18th century, the two main meals were a heavy breakfast accompanied by ale and a huge dinner—with nothing else between. The Duchess of Bedford (1788–1861) introduced the idea of afternoon tea, along with a friendly gossip and a walk in the fields. Afternoon tea, with bread and butter, sandwiches and cakes quickly became popular, especially with upper class ladies. The upper classes retained the practice of having a tea with snacks and cakes thereafter, while the working classes incorporated tea drinking with their evening meal. There are still people all over Britain who refer to an evening main meal as their tea. The British soldiers who were stationed in India throughout the 19th century and the early 20th century chose tea as a pleasant alternative to beer. Oddly enough, history records that those soldiers who avoided beer altogether and who only drank tea suffered far more from heat exhaustion than those who drank at least some beer during the course of each day. This may have something to do with the salts and natural chemicals that are found in beer.

Russia and the countries that surround it are great tea-drinking nations and they like their tea in a glass with a special holder either "straight" or more usually, with lemon and sugar. Russian tea may be made in a teapot but it is often brewed in a decorated samovar. In 1618 the Chinese embassy in Moscow presented Czar Alexis with several crates of tea, and shortly after this a treaty was formed that allowed trading caravans to cross the border between Russia and China. The length of the journey and the high cost of transporting tea by pack animal meant that at first only the wealthy could afford to drink it. Gradually the

price came down, especially after the trans-Siberian railway was opened in 1900 and tea became the national drink of Russia— along with vodka.

Immigrants to North America came from both tea and coffee drinking heritages. The shortsighted English government of George III imposed ridiculous taxes on tea and other products and his government interfered in the lives of the colonists in other highly irritating ways. Eventually the Americans cried, "no taxation without representation," and began to fight for independence. On the 16th of December 1773, a group of Americans dressed as Red Indians clambered onto an English ship called the Beaver and threw its cargo of tea into Boston harbour. Although Americans continued to import tea from Holland and also from a few rogue English traders, these difficulties encouraged Americans to choose coffee over tea as their national drink. An American invented iced tea in 1904. Modern Americans are taking up tea drinking in larger amounts now, because they perceive it as a healthy alternative to coffee.

Most of the tea that is imported into western countries such as Britain and the USA nowadays comes from Kenya, with some still coming from the traditional sources of India and Sri-Lanka. In recent times Indonesia has started to export tea, while some is grown in Malaya and even in the north of Australia where the soil and climate suits the crop. Despite the fact that Robert Fortune's success at smuggling tea seeds out of China broke the Chinese monopoly of tea cultivation, China is still a major tea-growing country. China is also a major exporter of plain and flavored Chinese styles of tea, which differ from the Indian tea flavors that are so beloved of British and Irish tea drinkers.

The History of Coffee

3

Coffee trees occur naturally in what is now Ethiopia and a rather charming story from this area tells us how the drink was first discovered. At some point in time around 800 A.D. a goatherd called Kaldi noticed his goats eating the cherry-red coffee berries and subsequently dancing happily from one shrub to another. The goatherd tried the beans for himself and discovered the caffeine buzz that this early form of Ecstasy produced. A monk noticed Kaldi's cheerful frolicking and tried the beans out on the brothers, to find that the following night they were not only wakeful but also filled with "divine" inspiration.

Apparently other early Africans were in the habit of making wine from the beans, but coffee didn't turn into a hot drink until it reached Arabia. It was in Arabia around 1000 A.D. that roasted beans were first brewed and by the 13th century devout Muslims were drinking coffee in order to keep awake during long periods of prayer, and also to fuel themselves for dervish dancing. From that time, wherever Islam ruled coffee followed. Turkey became a major coffee importer and at one time Turkish law permitted a wife to divorce her husband for failing to keep the family coffeepot filled! The Arabians managed to keep the secret of coffee cultivation to themselves by parching or boiling the beans that they exported, which spoiled the beans for cultivation in other countries. However, a canny smuggler called Baba Budan strapped a few fertile seeds to his belly and smuggled them out into the wider world.

In 1615, a Venetian merchant introduced coffee to Europe, but little happened for a year. After this, the Dutch managed to obtain a smuggled coffee plant, which they took to Java for cultivation.

Coffee smugglers of the 17th century.

Coffee drinking became popular in Europe, so much so that in Prussia that King Frederick the Great banned it because it was affecting the sale of beer. A Dutch merchant sent Louis XIV a coffee tree for the Paris Botanical Garden, and several years later an enterprising French naval officer called Gabriel Mathiew de Clieu asked for a few clippings from the King's tree. Permission was denied to the young sailor but before he left on his next voyage he climbed over the wall of the gardens in the dead of night and smuggled a small plant out of the hothouse.

On his voyage to Martinique, a jealous passenger tried to take the small bush from de Clieu and in a rage, this man managed to tear off a branch. This might have been the end of the story because along the way, pirates attacked the ship, but the French successfully fought them off, then a storm almost sank it. When the weather improved, the ship slowed to the extent that drinking water had to be rationed, but the determined De Clieu gave half his water allowance to his precious plant. Eventually the tiny bush was planted and kept under armed guard, and a mere 50 years after its struggle for survival, approximately 18 million bushes were thriving in the French Caribbean colonies.

Gabriel De Clieu tends his precious coffee plant.

In 1727, the Emperor of Brazil decided that he wanted to grow coffee but he needed to find a resourceful rascal to obtain the requisite beans for him. He found just such a person in the shape of Colonel Francisco de Melo Palheta, who he then dispatched to French Guiana, ostensibly to mediate over a border dispute. The Colonel could see no way of taking seeds or cuttings from the heavily guarded growing areas, so he resorted to using his charms on the Governor's wife. The dashing young Colonel obviously succeeded, because in a result worthy of a story by Ian Fleming, at a state farewell dinner this romantic lady presented him with a bouquet of local flowers—among which were coffee seedlings! From these seedlings, the huge Brazilian crops came into being, and this turned coffee from a rich person's treat into a drink for everyone.

Tips and Techniques for Tea and Coffee

4

O lder people will consider it silly of me to include a section on tea making, but for the vast numbers of people who only know how to throw a tea bag in a cup and pour hot water on it, tea making has become a lost art.

How to Make Tea

You will need to equip yourself with a teapot and a packet of loose tea. It doesn't matter whether the teapot is china, glass or steel but you must choose one that doesn't have a filter inside, because you need some of the tea leaves to fall into the cup. It is unlikely that you will have a proper tea caddy around, so treat yourself to an inexpensive container that has a well-fitting lid. Don't use an old jar that has had other foodstuffs kept in it because residual smells will taint your tea.

Warm the teapot. Traditionally, this would have been done by keeping it on the warm part of a range or old-style oven or by keeping the pot on a trivet close to a coal fire. Nowadays it is probably best to pour some hot water into the pot, swill it around and then throw it out again when you are ready to make your tea. Fill your kettle with freshly drawn water—stale water loses its oxygen content, so only freshly drawn water will do. While the kettle is coming to the boil, empty out any water that you have used to warm your teapot and take the pot to the kettle. Put in the tea and then pour briskly boiling water over the leaves. Put the lid on the teapot and leave it to infuse for a few minutes. The amount of tea that you put into your pot will vary with the number of cups of tea that you want to make and also the strength of tea that you prefer. A good rule of thumb is to use one rounded teaspoonful per person. If you like strong tea, you must leave the tea to infuse for a while and you can use a tea-cosy to prevent it from becoming too cool. Don't use a strainer. You or your inquirer can add milk, sugar or sweeteners if desired, as this won't affect the outcome of the reading. If you and your inquirer prefer China tea, Earl Grey tea and speciality teas with or without a slice of lemon, that's fine.

When I was a child, I can remember arguments raging as to whether the milk or the tea should be put into the cup first. If the milk is put in first, the tea will mix together with the milk in an instant; if it is put in afterwards, the tea will need to be stirred. As it happens, the latter is correct and it is for this reason that a teaspoon should always be provided, whether the tea drinkers take sugar or not. Of course, as far as divination is concerned, it doesn't matter one bit whether one drinks tea with or without milk or sugar.

Any kind of tea can be used for tea-leaf reading and if you only have tea bags to hand, these can be snipped open so that the tea can be brewed in its loose form, but it will be difficult to keep such tiny tea shavings from getting into your mouth. It would be better to buy a packet of loose tea. If you want to experiment with the more exotic larger leafed teas such as Darjeeling, you can do so. Herbal or fruit-based teas will do, as long as there is something that can be left in the cup for the purpose of divination. By experimentation, you will soon discover which kind of tea best suits your purposes.

Tips for Reading

Here are some important tips relating to tea-leaf reading:

1. If two spoons are accidentally placed in one saucer, there will be news of twins.

2. If a spoon is accidentally placed upside down in a saucer, there will be news of a close relative becoming ill.

3. A single leaf floating on a full cup of tea means that the inquirer will come into money.

4. A single leaf that is stuck at the side of a full cup signifies news of a stranger entering the inquirer's life. Check to see whether this will come from the inquirer's immediate neighborhood or through friends or family members (i.e. close to the handle), or from afar (away from the handle).

5. If the leaves are piled against the side of the cup that opposes the handle, trouble is on the way. This is not of the inquirer's own doing and it will come without warning.

6. If the leaves are rounded up on the handle side, there may also be trouble, but this time the inquirer has nobody to blame but herself.

7. Letters of the alphabet should always be noted, as they often give the initial of a significant person.

8. Numbers represent time, such as minutes, hours, days or weeks, depending upon the inquirer's situation.

9. A stalk represents a person, often a stranger. A long, firm stalk suggests a man while a shorter, thinner one represents a woman. If the stalk is straight, the stranger will be honest; if it is bent, he or she will be fickle. Slanted stalks suggest unreliable or untrustworthy people. The color of

the stalk will give a clue to the coloring of the person's skin or hair.

10. Lucky signs are horseshoes, circles, rings, flowers, trees, animals and crowns and also the number seven. Triangles are thought to be lucky, but if they are found at the bottom of the cup with the apex pointing downwards, the luck will run out. A triangle with the apex pointing upwards denotes a legacy, a windfall or an important meeting connected with money.

11. Squares suggest protection or restriction. A dangerous symbol such as a knife or a gun surrounded by a square shows protection from a potentially harmful situation.

12. Crosses denote sadness or losses.

13. Mountains suggest efforts to be made and troubles that will be overcome.

14. Dots always symbolize money. If the dots are close to another symbol, read them in conjunction with it. For example, if a letter appears, this would be good news about money.

15. Lines mean journeys; if the lines are straight, the journey will be trouble free, if they are wavy, there will be uncertainty and difficulties en route.

16. Rings signify marriage or a committed relationship and a broken ring suggests a split or unhappiness in marriage. A double ring could signify two marriages but it can also denote a marriage that the inquirer rushes into and regrets later.

17. A bell is a sign of a wedding.

18. Clear symbols are better omens than muddied ones.

If your inquirer is keen to find a new lover, try this experiment for her. Take a clean, dry teaspoon and balance it over the rim of a cup and drip liquid into the spoon counting the drops as you go. The number of drops that fall before the spoon tumbles into the cup signals the number of years the inquirer has to wait before finding the right lover.

If you fancy iced tea for a change, this is how you make it. Make a pot of tea in the usual way, steep for three to five minutes and pour into a jug. Add evaporated milk and sugar to taste and pour the concoction over ice cubes. If you want leaves in the drink for reading purposes, use loose tea and don't strain it.

Tea Leaves Are Not Just for Reading!

Here are some useful home remedies and tips relating to tea:

1. When travelling in countries where the water supply is not clean, always boil your drinking water. While you are boiling the water, you might as well throw a tea bag into some of it and enjoy a quick cuppa!
2. If you are one of the many women who suffers from monthly cramps, try drinking a cup or two of chamomile tea or the lovely tasting raspberry tea.
3. For morning sickness or migraine, try peppermint tea.
4. Try a little ginger in your tea when you are down with a cold, a stomach upset or rheumatism.
5. An old cure for a colicky baby is to add a little Chamomile tea to the baby's milk.
6. Warm teabags make a great soother for tired eyes and

cold tea gives instant relief for sunburn. The same goes for sweat-rash, sun allergy or jellyfish stings, mosquito bites and even the small cuts that you can get when handling paper. In fact, any minor skin ailment is helped by the application of a used teabag.

7. The tannin in tea is wonderful for mouth ulcers or for a sore throat. Make up some strong tea and allow it to cool and then use it as a mouthwash or a gargle. Put a warm teabag directly on an ulcer for instant relief.

8. Breast feeding? Sore nipples? Try black tea in teabags. Drinking anything aids milk production, so a cup of tea can only help; then place the used teabags on your nipples.

9. If you have brown hair, chamomile tea and even ordinary tea can be used for an after-shampoo rinse, as this will make your hair shine. Some teas give a slight reddish tinge to brown hair but chamomile is great for black hair.

10. If you suffer from blocked pores, try holding your face over a bowl of hot tea for a while and then washing your face well and finally rinsing it thoroughly with cold water.

11. Smelly feet? Soak them for 20 minutes in a bowl of hot tea once a day for three days and once a week thereafter. A peppermint tea soak will revive tired or sore feet.

12. Put used tea and teabags on your compost heap or around your plants.

13. A few used teabags kept in the fridge will absorb strong odors.

Coffee

Most of the information that relates to the reading of tea leaves applies to coffee in exactly the same way. The ritual of turning the cup upside down and using the left hand to turn it three times towards the left is exactly the same. The location of events, the timing of events and the way the grounds are piled up or spread around the cup are also the same. Obviously, comments about tea stalks can't be translated to coffee but the bubbles that form in a coffee cup can be substituted in order to provide extra information. If for instance, the bubbles form a specific shape, use them to guide you intuitively towards a conclusion or look up the symbol for that shape in the dictionary of symbols.

Types of Coffee

Some people prefer to use the kind of fine grounds that are familiar to Greek, Turkish and Arab coffee-drinkers, while others prefer a coarser grind, which may be put through a filter or a cafetière. If you use a coffee-filter or cafetière or any other system that keeps the coffee grounds away from the coffee, simply take a half-spoonful of the filtered coffee grounds and toss them into the inquirer's cup of coffee so that there is some sediment left in the cup for interpretation purposes. Once again, you will have to experiment with different kinds of coffee before you find the method that works best for you.

Part Two

READING
THE CUP

How Does Cup Reading Work?

5

Cup reading works in much the same way as dream interpretation because the symbols that you notice in the cup will have something to say. For example, a ring indicates a marriage-type relationship and it doesn't take a super-brain to work out what a broken ring or two rings might mean. A symbol that looks like a castle indicates safety and security in some area of life. Some of the symbols in this book are less obvious, but these have been tried and tested over such a long period of time that we simply accept them as being indicative of the strange way in which messages of fate and destiny are passed to the cup reader.

The Basic Rules of Cup Reading

The basic rules apply whatever beverage is used. Use a proper cup rather than a mug and if your cup is somewhat wide and shallow, so much the better. Ensure that the inside of your cup has no pattern or decoration on it and that the surface is smooth rather than fluted or shaped. The cup doesn't need to be a white one; any color will do as long as it is easy to see the shapes made by the leaves or grounds. Before you hand your inquirer her drink, look at the surface to see if there are any stalks, leaves, grounds or bubbles visible. After your inquirer has finished drinking, ask her to swirl the remaining liquid around in the cup in an anticlockwise direction three times, using her left hand. Then ask her to place the cup upside down on to the saucer. If there is so much liquid in the cup that it is likely to wash the leaves or grounds out, provide your inquirer with an extra cup or bowl and ask her to gently drain some of the excess away without losing the solid matter.

Now either you or the inquirer should turn the cup three times in an anticlockwise direction, once again using the left hand. Once this has been done, hold it in both hands, turn the handle towards yourself and tune in.

Location and Timing of Events

The handle represents the inquirer herself, so any leaves or grounds in that area suggest events that will concern her personally. Symbols in the handle area also refer to home and family matters. The opposite side of the cup concerns the actions of strangers and to events that occur in some sphere of life that is away from the home and family. A salesman, an executive or an entrepreneur who makes new contacts on a regular basis will have more activity routinely going on away from the handle, while a housewife is more likely to find most of the activity around the home area. In some cases, activity away from the handle side signifies people or locations that are at a distance from the inquirer.

Symbols that point towards the handle represent people or matters that are approaching the inquirer, while symbols that point away from the handle suggest people or situations that are moving away. The bottom of the cup shows sorrows and disappointments, and this is especially true when there is liquid left in the bottom of the cup. The top of the cup shows joyful and happy news, if a symbol that appears at the top of the cup is not a pleasant one, the chances are that the problem won't be too great and that it will soon be over.

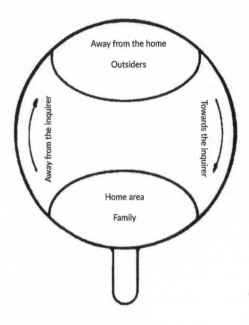

Fig 1. Location of Events

Some traditions suggest that the rim of the cup represents the near future, halfway down suggests events that will come about within a few months, while the area close to the bottom shows the distant future. If there are any numbers visible in the cup, this will help with the timing of events. A better tradition perhaps is to start at the handle and move towards the left. The area close to the handle shows the past and its bearing on the immediate situation, moving around the cup in a leftward direction brings the timing into the present and then onwards into the future.

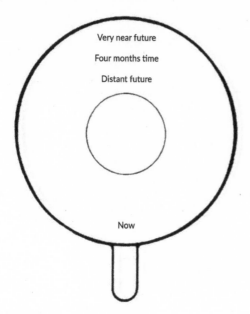

Very near future

Four months time

Distant future

Now

Fig 2. Timing of Events

Some traditions suggest that the happiest outcome of an event will occur if the symbol is found close to the rim of the cup, but if the same symbol is found at the bottom of the cup, sadness will result. A little tea left in the bottom of the cup represents tears.

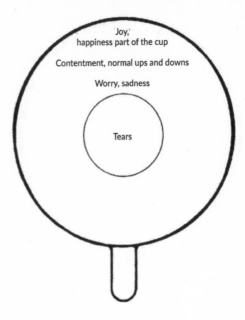

Joy,
happiness part of the cup

Contentment, normal ups and downs

Worry, sadness

Tears

Fig 3. How the Events Feel

Remember that if you have a vivid dream and you want a quick interpretation and you don't happen to have a dream dictionary to hand, you can use this book for a quick answer. A proper in-depth dream interpretation would be the correct approach but in an emergency, this book will give a surprisingly effective idea of what is behind your dream.

Psychic Ability

Many people ask me, "Do you need to be psychic to read tea cups?"

You don't need to be psychic for this kind of divination but it is helpful to have the kind of "eye" that can see patterns, images and shapes in a cup. If you have any latent psychic gifts or if you are naturally intuitive, you will find your talents increasing the more you use them. While cup reading may not strike you as the best way to develop your ESP, it works as well as any other method. This is due to the fact that anything that focuses your mind in a disciplined way while at the same time allowing you a form of free-wheeling association of ideas is at the heart of creative visualization.

There are highly developed clairvoyants who can tune in to an object that a person has worn in order to create a psychic link; this form of work is called psychometry. When an inquirer holds a cup and drinks from it, she leaves a little of her own vibrations or perhaps a trace of her aura on it, and this will help an intuitive cup reader to create a link with the inquirer. It might be worth asking your inquirer to hold the cup in her hands rather than simply to hold the handle (after the drink has sufficiently cooled) as this would boost any psychic transference.

A Personal Story

I have been an astrologer, palmist, Tarot reader and psychic for many years and during this time I have had dozens of readings given to me by other professionals, but none of them has ever used tea or coffee as a medium for their work. However, the

"Tales of the tea-leaves": an illustration from a 1914 issue of *The Century*.

very first reading that I ever had took place when I was about nine years old and this was indeed an old-style tea cup reading. I remember it clearly. I was visiting a neighborhood friend and the day was dull and wet, which meant that my friend and I couldn't play outside. As we were beginning to become rather bored and irritable, my friend's mother decided to cheer us up with a cup of tea and slice of cake. When we finished our drinks, she proceeded to read each of our cups.

I don't remember what she told my friend, Jeanette, but I will never forget her words to me. She told me that I would have a very up-and-down life with many changes. I would travel a great deal; I would write books. She was emphatic that despite the many ups and downs of my life that I would not spend my old age in poverty. Oddly enough, many other consultants have told me much the same thing in readings over the years, and it is a comforting thought to have confirmation of a pleasant old age.

Interpreting What You See

6

You will find a number and variety of symbols in the tea leaves and coffee grounds, and the next chapter will provide a dictionary of the most common symbols and their usual interpretation. However many symbols will be non-pictoral, such as astrological symbols and numbers.

Astrological Symbols

Astrological symbols become very powerful tools when combined with other symbols. For instance, a letter with an Aries symbol close by would suggest news of a new enterprise, while if it had a Taurus symbol close by, it might relate to money, goods, land, property or possessions. The astrological symbol could also refer to a person who is born under the sign that is shown in the cup.

Aries

Start of an enterprise. Self-motivation, courage and optimism. Blind faith and foolishness. Leaping into something new without looking.

Taurus

Sorting out priorities and personal values. Matters relating to money, possessions and ownership. Beauty, culture, art and music. Matters relating to building, property and land.

Gemini

Neighbors and local matters. Local travel and transport. Communications and documents. Business, especially sales. Sport and education. Brothers and sisters.

Cancer

Home, security and family. Mother figures. One's own business, especially shops or enterprises that are run from one's home. Emotions and moods. Caring for others, including care for animals.

Leo

Children, romantic lovers. Creative projects, pastimes, hobbies and some sports and games. Holidays and fun. Pride in achievement—either one's own or one's children's achievements.

Virgo

Work, duties to employers and employees. Health and hospitals. Food and nutrition. Clothing. Selection, choice, discrimination.

Libra

Partnerships and co-operation. Marriage or other steady relationships. Open enemies. Beauty, culture and food. New joint business enterprises.

Scorpio

Commitments, firm relationships. Joint finances. Birth, death, sex and all deep matters. Psychic and mediumistic matters. Matters related to the Police and medicine—especially surgery.

Sagittarius

The law. Philosophy and religion. Higher education. Travel, freedom and a lack of commitment. Matters related to large animals, especially horses.

Capricorn

Public life, status and positions of responsibility. Aims and ambitions. Career and work, especially big business. Struggle and effort that is worthwhile in the long term. Help from those in authority. Father figures.

Aquarius

Friends, detached relationships. Group activities, clubs and societies. Education. Astrology. Computers and other modern technology. Pride, courage but also arrogance. Hopes and wishes.

Pisces

Creativity. Mysticism. Private life, private sorrows. Self-sacrifice. Secret enemies. Dreams and desires, illusion and delusion. Mood changes that come from a shift in one's consciousness. Association with places of confinement. Loss of identity.

Tarot Symbols

Wands (or Staves)

Enthusiasm, new ventures, new people coming into the inquirer's life. Problems that can be overcome. Travel for pleasure, creativity of an intellectual kind. Business matters, especially marketing.

Cups

Emotional matters, love, marriage, family life. The past. Creation of beautiful things.

Swords

Troubles, illness, swift action to be taken. Quarrels and separations. Endings that pave the way for a fresh start. Courageous creativity that comes from new ideas. Help from professional people.

Pentacles (or Coins)

Money matters, practicalities, property and land, possessions. Business, finance and the start or completion of large-scale projects. Personal values. Creativity of a practical kind.

Playing Card Symbols

Clubs

Good luck, especially concerning money. New enterprises which will work out well for the inquirer. Helpful people around the inquirer. Education.

Diamonds

Money, a win. Sometimes the gift of a ring, possibly indicating a marriage to come. Practicalities, especially where money is concerned. A letter bringing good news.

Hearts

Happiness and abundance. Marriage and homelife. The birth of a child or the beginning of a creative enterprise. Satisfaction and completion.

Spades

Troubles, arguments, losses, bad luck and sadness. This could indicate the end of a relationship. Death of a situation that clears the way for a fresh start. Health problems for the inquirer or his/her family.

Numbers

One

Similar to the zodiac sign of Leo. A sign of creativity that might foretell the birth of a baby, or the birth of a project of some kind. Could also mean a holiday, family celebrations or a love affair on the horizon.

Two

Like the zodiac sign of Cancer. This may tell of a move of house or work to be done on the inquirer's present home. There may be news concerning older females in the family. Security will be important.

Three

Similar to the zodiac signs of Aries and Scorpio. This suggests efforts to be made in the near future. The inquirer will have to take a bold step forwards but should be warned against losing his/her temper or having silly accidents.

Four

Similar to the zodiac signs of Gemini and Virgo. This concerns communications, so the inquirer can expect important letters soon or news about neighbourhood matters. Work and services to be done, especially those requiring concentration, will be important, as will health matters.

Five

Like the zodiac sign of Sagittarius. This could mean legal matters to be settled soon. A long journey over water is a possibility, as is anything that will broaden the inquirer's mind.

Six

Like the zodiac signs of Taurus and Libra. This suggests that beauty and harmony are going to be important soon. There could be an interesting hobby involving the creation of beautiful things or there could be a romance on the way.

Seven

Like the zodiac sign of Capricorn. Serious matters may need to be attended to soon. There could be dealings with people in positions of authority. The inquirer's work will be important soon, as will his public image and status.

Eight

Similar to the zodiac sign of Aquarius. This shows an increasing level of independence on behalf of the inquirer. Possibly an increase of originality or a lack of convention in his/her future life.

He/she could behave in an uncharacteristic manner for a while. Unexpected events and upheavals could occur.

Nine

Like the zodiac sign of Pisces. This could bring romance, inspiration and immense kindness from others, but it could also bring muddles, illusion and bad judgement in an important matter.

A Dictionary
of Common
Symbols

7

Acorn

The start of something that is destined to grow to maturity and success, also a long life and good fortune. If this is in the middle of the cup, it indicates an improvement in health while other positions suggest that the inquirer's finances will improve.

Acrobat

A period of ups and downs.

Airplane

A sudden journey for the inquirer or for someone close to her. If the aeroplane is ascending, things are looking up but if it is descending, there will be trouble ahead. If the plane is travelling towards the inquirer, there will be visitors from afar.

Alligator

Treachery, rivals, secret enemies lying in wait.

Almond

Virginity, purity, possibly a Virgoan person.

Ambulance

Illness—if close to the handle, this will be a family matter.

Anchor

A hopeful sign of wishes coming true. Near the rim, success in career plus true love. Halfway down, a successful journey. If there are dots around the anchor, this will be very lucky indeed. If at the bottom of the cup, the inquirer can rely upon his friends to help her overcome difficulties. Only if the symbol is partially covered can it indicate continued problems.

Angel

Good news. Love, happiness and peace. Any new project, especially the birth of a child, will be lucky. If near the handle, domestic life will be happy.

Ant

Success through perseverance. Many difficulties before the goal is achieved.

Anvil

Concentration and hard work result in success. Stability, practicality and strength.

Arc

Ill health that threatens plans.

Arch

A happy marriage, a fresh start, unexpected benefits. A temporary situation becomes permanent.

Apple

Achievement, happiness and success. Hopes and wishes will be fulfilled. If at the bottom of the cup, temptation or overindulgence.

Arm

A sign of protection or perhaps an offer on the way. If the arm is holding a weapon, enemies are about.

Army

The inquirer will be involved in a stirring event.

Arrow

A message bringing bad news. If the arrow points towards the cup handle, bad news coming to the inquirer. If it points away, the inquirer could be the carrier of bad news to someone else. Dots show that the trouble is financial.

Axe

Difficulties—but this means that it is time to wield power and clear out dead wood. Sometimes a "battle-axe" type will enter the inquirer's life. Danger.

Baby

A baby may be born into the inquirer's family soon, especially if the baby is near the handle. Could mean the birth of a new idea or project, but if this is at the bottom of the cup, the plans will miscarry. Generally speaking, the problems are minor ones.

Bag

If closed, the inquirer will be caught in a trap. If open, she will escape.

Bagpipe

Disappointment. Possibly a visit to Scotland.

Ball

Ups and downs in life but the inquirer will bounce back. Great strides forward are possible. A desire to move house.

Ball and chain

Commitments, obligations. If at the bottom of the cup, these are onerous. A knotted chain suggests entanglements; a broken chain suggests breaking free.

Balloon

Success in life. If near the rim, this will come early; if halfway up the cup, success in middle age, but if near the bottom, success will come late in life.

Banana

Good luck and happiness.

Banner

Honors, fame and success. Marriage to a successful partner.

Barrel

Changing financial circumstances. A broken or empty barrel suggests financial hardship and setbacks but a complete barrel denotes good fortune and happiness ahead.

Basin

Tread water for a while. Trouble or illness for a woman close to the inquirer.

Basket

The birth of a child, social success, a pleasant surprise, good fortune in and around the home. Usually a good omen, but an empty basket or one obscured by other omens indicate domestic troubles.

a)   If near the rim, money and luck.
b)   Near the handle, a new baby.
c)   Flowers in the basket, happiness and fun.
d)   Dots around the basket, money coming soon.

Bat

Either false friends or a gift, good wishes and a long life. More than one bat, great good luck.

Bayonet

Danger, accidents, cuts, burns, etc.

Beans

 Money worries.

Bear

A long journey or a reassuring person entering the inquirer's life. Also a warning of misfortune.

Bed

A neat bed denotes a tidy mind, rest and peace but sexual activity can also be indicated. A rumpled bed speaks of sleepless nights and worry.

Bee

Social and financial success plus social gatherings.

a) Near the handle, family gatherings and celebrations in the home. Visitors bringing gifts and interesting news.

b) A small business to be launched.

c) Approaching the handle, a welcome guest.

d) Away from the handle, a swarm of bees suggests business meetings, seminars, conferences and exhibitions that will have a good outcome.

e) Money, success and honor are on the way; the inquirer could soon be addressing an audience.

f) If at the bottom of the cup, the inquirer will be subject to criticism or unfair allegations.

Beehive

Much activity at work, success and wealth from business.

Beetle

Money coming but also scandal.

Bell

Important news is on the way. If attached to a rope, a wedding.

a) Near the rim, promotion.

b) Halfway up, good news.

c) Near the bottom, sad news.

d) A hand-bell suggests that a public announcement will benefit the inquirer.

e) Two bells, great happiness and celebrations. A successful romance or marriage.

Bellows

Something that has died down will be fanned into life again.

Bird

Good news, good luck. If the wings are extended, this is a very good omen.

a) Birds flying can indicate travel, also good ideas that can be translated into money.

b) Surrounded by a circle or a square, a proposal.

c) Standing birds, plans held up.

d) Birds in a group, talks, discussions, business meetings.

e) In a cage, obstacles, restrictions. If the door is open, freedom is imminent.

f) If holding a branch, making up after an argument, a compromise solution.

f) With leaves nearby, good companions.

Bird's nest

Security, stability, affection, happy family life. Eggs in a nest can indicate children or a nest egg to come. Broken nest, a broken home.

Boat

Protection from danger, a safe refuge. A journey that teaches the inquirer something. A capsized or broken boat suggests danger, unreliable people and upsetting circumstances.

Bomb

Danger. A potentially explosive situation.

Book

a) If the book is closed, studies, research or a new skill to be learned.

b) Closed book: a secret, something needs to be investigated.

c) Open book: success, especially in legal matters.

d) An open person who brings pleasant surprises.

e) Marriage to a writer if a stalk is near the book.

f) Book and pen, the inquirer will write for a living.

Boomerang

Gossip, false friends. If the inquirer gossips, this will rebound on her. An unprincipled past action will rebound.

Boot

a) Changing situations or moves are afoot. If the boot is near the handle, the changes will be in the home area; if away from the handle, they will be in public or social life.

b) Loss of a job, getting the boot.

c) Pair of boots, protection from pain or loss.

d) Pair of boots, business that involves travel, sales, deliveries, etc., will be successful.

Bottle

Either bottles of medicine on the way or opening a bottle in celebration.

Bouquet

Celebrations, joy, success and prosperity. Parties and weddings. A good omen for a new relationship, a happy marriage or a new venture. Dreams will come true.

Bow and arrow

Bad news, spite, jealousy, rumors, slander.

Box

If open, a romantic problem will sort itself out; if closed, something that is lost will soon be found.

Branch

Time to branch out.

Bricks

Steady growth, good foundations.

Bridge

The way to success is open.

Broom

Time to clear away old problems and make a clean sweep, because new initiatives are ahead. Can be a sign of marriage (jumping the broomstick).

Buckle

Defence and protection. Partnerships will be successful.

Bugle

Time to speak up and to raise one's level of visibility. The inquirer should gather his strength for a tough project ahead.

Bull

a) Important contact with Taurean person.

b) Strength and power for a good purpose

c) Arguments and bad feeling. The direction the bull is facing will show whether this is coming to or from the inquirer.

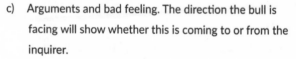

Bulldog

Tenacity.

Buoy

Hope and help.

Bush

New friends and new opportunities.

Buttercup

Desire for wealth—look around for other signs to see if this will actually materialize.

Butterfly

Fickle lover, a short-lived affair. If surrounded by dots, the inquirer will also waste money. Other interpretations see this as a symbol of happiness and pleasure.

Cabbage

Jealousy or missed opportunities. With dots, jealousy at the inquirer's place of work.

Cactus

Courage and stoicism.

Caduceus

This is the winged staff that belongs to the Roman god, Mercury, who is associated with healing, communications, travel and magic. This suggests healing after a period of sickness or depression.

Cake

Celebrations, hospitality and parties.

Candle

a)   Help from others or inspiration given to others.

b)   Zeal for knowledge, enlightenment.

c)   Moth near the flame, a disastrous attraction.

d)   A guttering candle shows that someone close to the inquirer is becoming weaker in health or alternatively less important to the inquirer.

Candelabra

Sudden illumination, solution to problems.

Cannon

a) Good luck, help from powerful friends.

b) News from someone in the Forces.

c) Promotion, especially if there is a star nearby.

Cap

Discretion will be needed; the inquirer must be careful whom she trusts. Not a time for speculative ventures.

Car

Local travel or changing circumstances.

Castle

a) A strong or influential person will help the inquirer.

b) Security and safety, a good home life.

c) If the castle is ruined, ruined hopes and dreams.

d) An inheritance is possible.

Cat

If the cat is pouncing, there will be treachery, false friends. If seated, contentment and good luck.

Catapult

An unprovoked attack, a mugging, arguments and discord.

Cauldron

Sacrifices to be made.

Censer

Purification, prayer, hope and protection; also religious and other types of ritual. Patience will be needed if this is at the bottom of the cup.

Chain

A partnership, a commitment but if the chain is broken, a disappointment. Alternately, the inquirer is being advised to put his energies into work.

Chair

A visitor or a time to rest. With dots around, financial improvement.

Chariot

Energy, activity, dynamic events, success in business. Matters that will need control.

Cherry

Emotional awakening, first love. This is associated with the goddess Venus.

Chessmen

Concentration will be needed.

Chestnut tree

Justice.

Chicken

Easter time could be important to the inquirer. Pleasant new interests.

Child

May herald the birth of a child or of a child coming into the life of the inquirer. Alternative, successful new ventures and creative enterprises.

Chimney

If the smoke rises straight up, things will go well; if it goes sideways, there will be restriction and boredom. If there is no smoke, there will be hidden danger.

Christmas tree

Good luck around Christmas time.

Church

Help, safety, unexpected benefits. A legacy perhaps.

Cigar

New and influential friends. If the cigar is broken, a broken attachment or business losses.

Circle or ring

a)   A successful event, possibly a wedding.
b)   Circle with dots, a baby—three dots, a boy.
c)   Two circles, either a hasty marriage that brings regrets or two marriages.
d)   The completion of a project or the end of a phase.

Claw

Danger, enemies.

Clergyman

a)   Blessing, end of an argument.
b)   A religious ceremony, if within a circle, a wedding.
c)   Baby or child on the way or a christening.
d)   If at the bottom of the cup, a funeral.

Cliff

Danger, the inquirer needs to take care.

Clock

a) Improvement in health, work and money if near the rim.
b) Bottom of the cup, death.
c) Time to get on with things.
d) An influential or important meeting.

Clouds

Trouble, doubts unsolved problems.

Clover

Good luck is on the way.

Coach and horses

A rise in status, influential friends, a more upmarket home and lifestyle.

Coat

End of a partnership or friendship.

Cock

a) New beginnings, good news, an achievement but this may go to the inquirer's head.

b) Failure of plans if near the bottom of the cup. The inquirer shouldn't be too quick to crow about himself.

Coffin

A bad omen, sad news, regret, loss. May need to bring something to an end. Someone may part from the inquirer, but this may be a relief.

Column

a) Promotion, success, but a warning here against arrogance.

b) Help from friends.

c) Broken column, failure in business, relationships or health.

d) Broken column, an unfaithful friend.

Comb

Disloyalty, deceit.

Comet

Unexpected events, unexpected visitors.

Comma

Rest and relaxation are needed.

Compass

Change of direction. Travel.

Cork

Celebrations, parties.

Corkscrew

The inquirer will have to go about things in a roundabout way; she is also being warned against the deviousness of others.

Corn

Wealth, achievement, rewards, joy, fruition.

Cornucopia

The horn of plenty is a symbol of abundance, joy and fruition of plans. Good food and an easy life for a while.

Cot

A baby is coming.

Cow

Relaxation and a peaceful phase.

Crab

May indicate a Cancerian person entering the inquirer's life. Can also denote a devious enemy.

Crescent

a) New moon, new interest in life, success in financial affairs.
b) Journey over water.
c) Success through or for women.
d) Changes coming at the time of the new moon.
e) A wedding.
f) If this is an old moon, delays; patience will be needed.
g) Moon with star, exceptionally lucky.

Cricket bat

The inquirer will take up a sport soon or she could be a good sport.

Crook

Symbol of protection and leadership.

Cross

Troubles, suffering, worry and loss, also sacrifice. Illness around the inquirer, sad news soon if near the rim.

Crow

Ill health, especially if near the bottom of the cup.

Crown

Honors, success, rewards. With stars, luck out of the blue.

Cup

Success and fulfillment, especially in creative or emotional matters. A new friend.

Cupid

Love.

Curtain

Secrets.

Daffodil

A happy announcement or a good friend.

Dagger

A jealous person will make trouble, also a warning against haste or of trouble on the way.

Daisy

New love affair, happiness in marriage.

Dancer

Celebrations and joy, a wish will be granted.

Deer

Good omen for studying and taking exams, otherwise a quarrel.

Desk

A letter will bring good news.

Devil

Commitment to a course of action or a person. Alternatively a passionate and hectic love affair.

Dice

Warning not to gamble if clouds, daggers or other bad omens are nearby, otherwise speculation should be all right.

Diver

The inquirer may discover something soon or get to the bottom of things.

Dog

A faithful friend. If the dog is running and happy, there will be happy meetings, but if sad or near the bottom of the cup, a friend will help.

Dolphin

Safety while travelling; also help in an emergency.

Donkey

The inquirer will have to be patient and prepared to make a few sacrifices, especially if this is near the bottom of the cup, however this is also an optimistic sign. If near the rim of the cup, good luck, even an inheritance. Otherwise peace and happiness.

Dot

A single dot increases the importance of any symbol near it, otherwise dots mean money.

Dove

Peace, love and happiness. A good omen all round but probably most lucky in the domestic arena.

Dragon

Unforeseen problems, major clashes and upheavals that will need to be faced rather than avoided.

Dragonfly

Good news, good events in the home, this could mean household renovations.

Drum

Rows and arguments and if near the bottom of the cup, rumors and scandal. A successful career involving the general public, in which the inquirer will reach a position of power and influence. Also, the inquirer must expect a change.

Duck

Money coming, luck in speculation and any work connected with travel and foreigners.

Eagle

A move of house or a time to grasp opportunities. The inquirer should use his knowledge, skill and wit and make a concerted effort.

Ear

Interesting and unexpected news.

Earrings

Cross-purposes, misunderstandings.

Easel

A good omen for anyone engaged in creative work. Dots around the easel bring money.

Egg

A symbol of fertility and abundance. A good omen for the birth of a child or of a project.

Elephant

A symbol of strength, wisdom and a slow ascent to success. A good time to start a new business or a new relationship. A trustworthy friend is needed.

Envelope

Good news is on the way. A letter or number on the envelope may give a clue to whom from and when it will come.

Eye

a) Take care, watch out.

b) Protection from problems, vigilance.

c) Knowledge, intelligence and comprehension. A time when the inquirer's eyes may be opened.

Face

a) This can indicate changes for the worse.

b) If the face looks like someone the inquirer knows, she will see her soon.

c) If the face is smiling, the omen is good, if scowling or looking crafty, this warns of difficult people.

d) Friendships.

Falcon

The inquirer will rise to the top of the tree and become very successful.

Fan

A warning not to talk too freely. Could also indicate a flirtation.

Feather

Instability, unpredictability, lack of concentration.

Fence

Minor setbacks, hurdles to be crossed.

Fig tree

A lucky sign, plenty of goodies to come.

Figurehead

This could refer to a titular head of an organization or it could mean sailing into calmer waters.

Fir tree

Success in artistic work.

Fire

Artistic achievement but if at the bottom of the cup, a warning against haste.

Fire engine or fire extinguisher

Warnings against danger and haste.

Fireplace

Happiness in the home.

Fish

a) One of the very best omens. It indicates luck in anything that the inquirer is doing or wants to do.
b) Travel or a move of house or a lucky encounter with a foreigner.
c) Two fishes that are tied are a symbol of Pisces so this could refer to a Piscean person.

Flag

Some very different meanings here:

a) Danger threatens, especially if the flag is dark, the inquirer must be alert.

b) Good news or good fortune if appearing with good omens.

c) Death of a king or a ruler of some kind, especially if the flag is at half-mast.

d) Time to put on a good front, be courageous, and go for it!

Flask

Rest and refreshment.

Flower

A wish will be granted. Honors. Love or marriage if on the side of the cup; on the bottom, an unhappy love affair.

Fly

A minor irritation, a swarm of flies, many minor annoyances.

Foot

Good news after a while.

Forest

A muddle, too much concentration on details, too many people wanting something of the inquirer.

Forget-me-not

The inquirer either cannot forget someone or she wants someone to remember her.

Fork

a) False friends, beware of flattery.
b) New interests if the fork is pointing upwards; old problems reappearing if it is pointing downwards.
c) This can also point to a choice of pathways to follow.

Fork in the road

Two possible pathways forward.

Fort

The inquirer will soon be in a strong position.

Fountain

Joy, satisfaction and happiness. This also indicates sex and the forces of life.

Fox

A cunning and deceitful person.

Frog

A number of meanings here

a) A move of house or premises.
b) Avoid self-indulgence and vanity.
c) Associated with the goddess Isis, this foretells a change in the inquirer's life that will bring happiness, good health, good friends, love, fruitfulness and protection from harm.

Fruit

Abundance, prosperity, happiness and success.

Gallows

Bad luck. The inquirer's judgement may not be good but neither will the judgement of those who want to hurt the inquirer be any good either.

Garland

Achievement, honors, happiness in relationships.
If at the bottom of the cup, a funeral.

Gate

An unexpected opportunity, a change of a lifetime.

Gauntlet

A challenge.

Geese

Invitations to social events, but there may be unwelcome
visitors.

Giant

A strong person or a strong influence.

Giraffe

A lack of thought or tact may cause trouble.

Gladioli

Victory and achievement, a bold step forward. Possibly a visit to Australia or an Australian connection.

Glass

Honesty, principle, integrity.

Glove

A challenge.

Goat

A person born under the sign of Capricorn, alternatively enemies.

Goblet

Same as cup.

Golf club

Sports may be important soon or business mixed with pleasure.

Gondola

Travel and romance.

Grapes

Various meanings here

a) Grapes are associated with the Roman god Bacchus or the Greek god Dionysos (Dionysius) and therefore talk of wine and revelry, but these gods can be deceptive and dangerous, so the inquirer is warned not to allow things to go to his head.

b) A sick person will be better soon

c) Pleasant romantic involvement.

d) Visit to a hospital.

e) Great happiness that will last.

Grass

Time to make oneself useful.

Grasshopper

a) The inquirer should keep the right track and avoid jumping from one thing to another.

b) A friend who has been away will return.

Grave

Similar to coffin.

Greyhound

Symbolic of speed, thus a time to forge ahead and make a success of things, also a good time to speculate.

Guitar

Social events that include music. Romance, even a chance of being serenaded!

Gun

Quarrels, anger, violence, war, even death by violence. If the gun is in the home area, that is where the danger will be, otherwise mugging and assault are possible. If the gun is at the bottom of the cup, there is a real threat of death as a result of war.

Ham

A time of plenty, good social life, parties and happy events in the home.

Hammer

Work to be done, not all of it pleasant, but it needs to be done. The inquirer may need to be ruthless.

Hammock

Time to relax.

Hand

Many meanings to this one:
  a) Look to see where the hand is pointing to see where a situation will develop (e.g. near the handle = in the home).
  b) If the hand is open, a good, helpful friend.
  c) If the fingers are closed but the thumb protruding, protection and safety.
  d) Thumbs up, go ahead now.
  e) Thumbs down, wait.
  f) A fist denotes quarrels, resentment and enemies around.
  g) Clasped hands, friendship, an agreement.
  h) A clenched fist at the bottom of the cup shows that the inquirer will have to keep his feelings and emotions under tight control.

Handcuffs

Problems, possibly being in a situation not of the inquirer's choosing.

Hand mirror

Prophetic dreams, enlightenment.

Hare

Shyness and timidity. A time to be bolder. Could represent a shy friend who needs help if at the bottom of the cup.

Harp

The inquirer will have a happy marriage. If single, a lovely romance is on the way. The inquirer will never want for money.

Hat

A man's hat is supposed to be unlucky while a woman's one is a fortunate sign. May be the sign of a visitor or a social event that would require a hat, such as a wedding or a christening. If the hat is bent or broken, plans will fall through; if at the bottom of the cup, there could be a rival coming into the inquirer's life. Another interpretation suggests being crowned with honor.

Hatchet

Same as axe.

Hawk

Trouble caused by a jealous person.

Hawthorn

If in the handle area, problems in the home, if away from the handle area, luck in romance, plus prosperity to the inquirer and his loved-ones.

Heart

a) A symbol of love, a lover or a good friend and confidante.
b) Hearts with arrows through them, a passionate romance.
c) Other marks bring extra happiness, e.g. dots—money, circle—a wedding, a heart with small leaves nearby means marriage to a wealthy partner. Two hearts close together plus small leaves, a lover's tiff.
d) If at the bottom of the cup, there may be health problems—possibly heart trouble.

Heather

Good luck and promises that are kept.

Helmet

Either a battle or a passionate love affair—or both.

Hen

Happiness in the home, female visitors.

Hill

Obstacles to progress, especially if clouds are also seen.

Hoe

Hard work will be rewarded.

Holly

Good luck around Christmas time.

Honeysuckle

Love and affection that will last.

Horn

A sign of prosperity.

Horse

a) A galloping horse denotes good news on the way.

b) A rider on a horse brings good news from far away.

d) A horse's head indicates a faithful lover to come. If surrounded by dots, the lover will be wealthy.

e) Clouds around the horse's head, delays in romance, but this should be all right in the end.

Horse and cart

A move of house or business premises. If the cart is loaded, the move is good; if the cart is empty, the move could be due to losses.

Horseshoe

Good luck, good health, money coming.

Hourglass

Decision time is here.

House

a)   If near the handle, domestic strife.
b)   If near the rim, a move to a better home or business premises.
c)   A change for the better. For lovers, a wish will come true.
d)   On the side of the cup, a temporary move or a holiday.
e)   Cloudy and/or at the bottom of the cup, care will be needed in business and personal life.

Human figure

Take note of surrounding symbols for clues.

Iceberg

Danger.

Initials

This refers to people who will influence the inquirer's life.

Insect

Minor worries, soon to be overcome.

Iris

An interesting message.

Iron

Problems can be ironed out, others will co-operate.

Island

A place to retreat to, an enjoyable holiday.

Ivy leaf

Reliable friends.

Jester

Parties and fun with amusing friends. Also a fresh start but with a warning not to make a fool of oneself.

Judge

A time to weigh things up.

Jug

Near the rim, good health; near the bottom, extravagance causing losses. Other positions indicate power, prosperity and a raise in status.

Juggler

This could indicate a new job or a promotion at work. The inquirer will use his skills and talents successfully. Salesmanship and marketing will be needed but there is a warning not to be taken in by others.

Kangaroo

Home life will be good.

Kettle

Near the handle, comfort and contentment in the home; if accompanied by clouds or unpleasant omens, discord in the home and a need for the inquirer to strive to put this right. Bottom of the cup, domestic problems and ill health.

Key

a)   A move of house or premises.

b)   If near the bottom of the cup, robbery is possible.

c)   A passionate affair.

d)   Crossed keys, a position of honor and authority, also success in romance.

e)   Bunch of keys indicates health, wealth and happiness in love.

f)   Can be a symbol of increasing enlightenment and new interests.

Keyhole

A lucky omen for love and sex but frustration if at the bottom of the cup.

King

A powerful friend and improvements at work.

Kite

A wish will be granted. The inquirer should go ahead with schemes but with a realistic attitude and she should not take chances.

Knapsack

Near the rim, a fortunate journey; if near the bottom, it would be better to wait.

Kneeling person

Time to pray for guidance. Perhaps submission to others.

Knife

An unlucky sign showing quarrels and separations.

a) Near the handle, a broken home.
b) Away from the handle, a stab in the back—possibly at work.
c) Bottom of the cup, legal matters going wrong.
d) A knife anywhere can foretell surgery, injections, or dental treatment.
e) Crossed knives, violence; broken knife, impotence, helplessness.

Knight in armor

A strong person will help the inquirer. If the inquirer is female, this could herald a new lover.

Lace

A lucky sign, improvements are on the way.

Ladder

a) Spiritual enlightenment, prophetic dreams.

b) Advancement, promotion.

c) Missing rungs, setbacks but not failure.

d) At the bottom of the cup, financial misfortune.

Ladle

Working partnerships will go well.

Ladybug

Money worries will pass, a windfall.

Lamb

If near the handle or facing it, plenty of food and drink in the home. Otherwise no particular shortage of necessities.

Lamp

a)   Financial success.

b)   Near the rim, a celebration soon.

c)   Near the handle, a discovery in the home.

d)   Finding things out or finding things that have been lost.

e)   Bottom of the cup, celebrations will be postponed.

f)   Two lamps show that the inquirer will be married twice.

Leaf

News, good luck, a turn for the better. A good sign for future prosperity.

Lemon

Something turns sour, others may be jealous or bear grudges.

Letter

News. The position of the letter will show if the news is good or not. If dots nearby, money will come. If a heart is nearby, there may be emotional or marital problems.

Lighthouse

Trouble can be averted, hidden dangers will be revealed.

Lines

A good time to progress but the position of the lines and any other signs around them need to be taken into account. Wavy lines suggest uneven progress.

Lion

Strong and influential friends. Someone born under the sign of Leo could soon become important to the inquirer.

Lizard

The inquirer should hesitate to believe all she is told. Treachery is in the air.

Loaf of bread

Plenty of good food and money, end of money worries.

Log

If lighted, warmth and companionship; if unlit, wasted opportunities.

Loom

The pattern of events will soon emerge.

Loop

Impulsive actions causing problems.

Luggage

A journey, large luggage or a lot of it may indicate emigration. Luck through travel.

Lute/lyre

Success in music and the arts and parties at home. Perhaps sadness in romance.

Magnet

The inquirer will be drawn to things that are good for her.

Man

a) If facing towards the handle, a visitor. If the man is distinct, he will be dark haired, if not, he will be pale in coloring.
b) With an arm outstretched, she will bring gifts.
c) If facing away from home, he could be leaving.
d) Carrying bags, a hard-working man.
e) Look for initials to discover his name.

Mansion

Rise in status, a rich partner.

Map

Travel, also a choice of routes open to the inquirer.

Maple leaf

Don't waste opportunities now. Could indicate a pleasant event in the autumn or a contact with Canada.

Mask

Parties and celebrations. Sometimes sign that someone is out to deceive the inquirer and that she should be discreet.

Maypole

A sign of fertility and abundance. An indication that the spring brings a change for the better.

Medal

A reward.

Melon

Prosperity, a happy event, good news.

Mermaid

Seduction either by a person or an enticing situation. Someone may be nice to the inquirer's face but nasty behind his back, also temptation of some kind.

Meteor

Like the comet, this can indicate a sudden rise in status or a successful venture but care will be needed to ensure that it doesn't fizzle out.

Michaelmas daisy

Reunion, also an indication of good times around the end of September.

Minister

See clergyman.

Mirror

See hand-mirror.

Mistletoe

Love at Christmas time, otherwise problems will soon pass.

Mole

An enemy could undermine the inquirer's position, or there may be something yet to be revealed.

Monk

Religious and spiritual matters will become important. A time for retreat, contemplation, inward journeys and rest.

Monkey

A flattering person who wishes to harm the inquirer. Guard against gossip.

Monkey puzzle tree

Time to get rid of objects and people that are jinxed or unlucky for the inquirer.

Monster

Inner fears will rise up.

Moon

a) A love affair.

b) If obscured by other leaves, depression or emotional stress.

c) If in the first quarter, new projects.

d) If in the last quarter, the inquirer's luck is running out.

e) Surrounded by dots, a relationship or marriage based on money.

Moth

A dangerous attraction, leading to unhappiness.

Mountains

a) Great goals but obstacles will need to be overcome.

b) If the peaks are clear, the inquirer will be able to clear away obstacles.

c) With dots, hard work brings financial rewards.

d) If upside down, frustration.

Mouse

Timidity could result in missed opportunities. Poverty or theft,
especially if at the bottom of the cup.

Mouth

The inquirer will hear something to his advantage.

Mug

Visitors, a celebration.

Mule

Patience will be required but the inquirer should not be too stubborn.

Mushroom

a) Business setbacks or trouble in the home.
b) Expansion of horizons.
c) A home in the country.
d) Expansion of awareness and sensitivity, beginning of enlightenment, psychic awakening.
e) Illusion, delusion, drug-induced ailments.

Music

Good luck.

Nail

Either an injustice or a sudden illness.

Necklace

Love ties will be important. These are successful if the necklace is complete but a breakup if the necklace is broken.

Needle

The inquirer will be admired for his achievement.

Net

A safe ending to a period of anxiety.

Nettle

The inquirer will overcome a tough problem by using courage.

Nun

Spiritual guidance, perhaps a good female friend who offers advice.

Nurse

Illness.

Oak-tree

Strength and courage, also building something durable. Health, wealth and happiness in marriage.

Oar

Help from others.

Octopus

Entanglement, a messy situation.

Onion

The inquirer must take care that secrets or confidential information are not leaked.

Orchids

The start of a passionate affair. If the orchids are at the bottom of the cup, this will be destructive.

Organ

A religious ceremony.

Ostrich

No point in burying one's head in the sand. Also travel, getting away from it all for a while.

Owl

Gossip, scandal and allegations. Possible trouble resulting from the death of a friend or a relative.

Padlock

If open, a surprise; if closed, a warning.

Pail

The inquirer will have to clear up a few things before starting anything new.

Palace

A raise in status and financial position. Marriage for money.

Palm tree

Success, honor, respect for the inquirer, his family and his children.

Panther

Treachery and disloyalty from a trusted associate.

Parachute

A lucky escape.

Parcel

A surprise, a gift.

Parrot

A journey or scandal and gossip.

Parsley

Some form of purification.

Pawnbroker's sign

Lean times ahead.

Peacock

a) With spread tail, buying land or premises.
b) If clear, good marriage, health, wealth and happiness.
c) Success, fame and fortune for the inquirer's children.
d) Success in one's career, a comfortable life.
e) Bottom of the cup, disappointment from children, plans not working out and a loss of dignity.
f) Bottom of the cup, illness.

Pear

A comfortable life with plenty of money.

Pen

The inquirer will have to write letters soon.

Pendulum

Changes in direction and/or time spent with easygoing friends and relaxation that banishes tension.

Penguin

Travelling south, or hearing from someone who lives to the south of the inquirer.

Penknife

Lack of co-operation, loosening of ties.

Pentagon

A balance between mind and body.

Pepper pot

Arguments caused by a manipulative person.

Pestle and mortar

Medication, treatment for illness.

Pheasant

A promotion, present or legacy but there may be a legal loss.

Phoenix

Recovery, rebirth. A lover could come back or a creative failure could be successfully reworked.

Pickaxe

Strikes and discord at work.

Pig

Material success at the expense of spiritual values.

Pigeon

News from abroad.

Pillar

See column.

Pineapple

Wishes will turn into reality.

Pipe

A problem will be solved, possibly with the aid of a kind man. Keep an open mind and don't suspect double-dealing where there is none.

Pistol

Danger.

Pitchfork

Muddles, accidents, arguments, violence.

Plait

The inquirer's life will be wrapped up with someone else's.

Plough

The start of a project that will require patience but that will be rewarded.

Policeman

Help from those in authority.

Poppy

The poppy has become part of our collective unconscious due to the waste of life in the poppy fields of Flanders during the First World War. It still retains the symbolism of unnecessary pain and loss, especially as a result of war. Traditionally this symbol also means pain, loss, sadness and illness, especially if at the bottom of the cup.

Postman

Important news. If near the rim, swift news; near the bottom, delays in communications.

Posy

A happy and fortunate symbol; romance, love. If a ring or a bell is nearby, a wedding.

Profile

A new friend.

Pump

A generous nature.

Purse

Enough money coming in for comfort except when at the bottom of the cup where losses, expenses and theft occur. With dots, a profitable venture.

Pyramid

Increased spiritual awareness, achievements after hard work.

Queen

An influential and helpful woman unless at the bottom of the cup where she would be meddlesome and spiteful.

Question mark

Hesitancy, caution will be required.

Quill pen

Documents to be signed.

Rabbit

a)   The inquirer should try to overcome timidity.

b)   Amusements and fun, possibly around Easter time.

Rabbit's foot

Good luck, gambles should come off.

Rainbow

Happiness and prosperity. Look to see where the end of the rainbow falls: if in the home area, that is where the inquirer's luck will come from, otherwise she may be luckier outside the home.

Rake

a) Hard work and attention to details.
b) Outstanding business needs to be cleared up.
c) Sport or hobbies will go well.
d) Near the bottom of the cup, old grievances could be raked up.
e) If broken, a broken engagement.

Ram

Someone born under the sign of Aries will be important to the inquirer.

Rat

Treachery, deceit and loss. Friends or lovers could turn out to be rats.

Rattle

Children will bring joy.

Raven

Bad news. If at the bottom of the cup, news of illness, loss, sadness or a death.

Razor

Accidents, quarrels, danger, partings.

Reptile

Deceit and treachery, malice and hurt from those who the inquirer thought were friends.

Rider

News coming to the home, work or social area, depending upon which way the rider faces.

Ring

A marriage symbol. Look for a number or an initial near the ring to see who is involved. If at the bottom of the cup, a broken engagement.

Road

Two parallel lines that look like a road show that the inquirer's situation is about to change. If the lines are straight, the way forward will be easy, if they are wavy, there will be difficulties, but the goal can still be reached. If there is a fork in the road, choices will have to be made and a bend suggests unexpected events.

Robin

Oddly enough, the robin is an ancient symbol of death, so there could be a death around the inquirer. Alternatively, a situation could die away. Another interpretation states that there will be luck coming during the winter.

Rocket

Happy events, possibly marriage for one of the inquirer's children. The inquirer could fall passionately in love.

Rocks

Unseen danger but obstacles can be overcome.

Rolling pin

A busy time in the home but also arguments within the home.

Roof

A new home and/or a new relationship.

Rose

a) Great success in creative enterprises, also popularity.

b) A fortunate sign for love and marriage.

c) The name, Rose, will mean something soon.

d) If at the bottom of the cup, delays and setbacks in romance.

Rosemary

The inquirer is being asked not to forget someone.

Rudder

Fate guides the inquirer.

Ruined buildings

Shattered hopes but also a time to start over again.

Runner

Messages and news. If the accompanying symbols are fortunate, the news will be good but if the runner is obscured or at the bottom of the cup, the news will be sad.

Sack

An unexpected event.

Saddle

Changes, journeys, new opportunities.

Sailor

News from over water.

Sausages

Wining and dining. If near the handle, good times in the home.

Saw

Interfering friends and neighbors.

Scaffold

The inquirer must keep within the law.

Scales

A lawsuit. If the scales are balanced, all will be well; if they are uneven, there will be losses, or someone could do the inquirer an injustice.

Scepter

Honors and rewards; a position of authority.

Scissors

A separation, quarrels and misunderstandings. Look at the area of the cup to see where these occur.

Scorpion

A Scorpio person will soon be important to the inquirer.

Seagull

Storms ahead.

Seesaw

Ups and downs in fortunes but the end result should be all right.

Shark

Danger.

Shell

a) Good news, luck and money are on the way. This is fortunate for relationships too.
b) If the inquirer is fighting an injustice or a legal matter, there will be a good outcome.
c) A sign of rebirth, spiritual awareness and a change of consciousness.

Shepherd

Someone will guide, help and take care of the inquirer. With sheep, good fortune.

Ship

A lucky journey, especially if it is concerned with business, good news from abroad.

Shirt

A generally good sign but if this is obscured, loss by speculation.

Shoe

A change for the better.

Sickle

Death or sorrow around the inquirer.

Signpost

Look to see where this is pointing and interpret the symbols that you see there because these will be especially important. Also, advice or direction.

Skeleton

Financial losses can be expected or there may be the loss of a friend. A spell of ill health. Skeletons will emerge rather embarrassingly from the cupboard.

Skull and crossbones

A rip-off, a highjack!

Snake

Hatred and enmity, plots by or against the inquirer.

Soldier

Either a powerful ally or hostility and people ganging up against the inquirer—or both.

Spade

Hard work with successful results.

Sparrow

a)   If the inquirer is short of money this will soon change.

b)   Oddly enough, this sign can warn of a death, especially a strange one such as murder by a nonentity or some kind of mystery disappearance.

Spider

A determined and persistent character who is also crafty. A warning of something that is going on in secret or of a secret plot. Reward for hard work.

Spire

Spiritual attainment and a rise in status.

Spoons

The inquirer's family will help her out. Also, one spoon, a birth; two, a proposal of marriage.

Square

Restrictions and hardships but also protection from long-term loss or harm.

Squirrel

Save for a rainy day.

Stag

A vigorous young man, if the inquirer is female, a strong young lover is on the way.

Stairs

A rise in status or spiritual enlightenment.

Star

A variety of meanings here:

    a)   Six-pointed, good fortune, fulfillment of dreams.

    b)   Five-pointed, an increase of spiritual awareness.

    c)   Small stars near the handle suggest talented children.

    d)   Large numbers of stars suggest problems, loss or grief, but finances will be all right in the end.

    e)   A single star near the bottom of the cup is a warning to change direction before all is lost.

Sticks

These represent people and the shape and coloring will represent
their appearance.

a) Crossed sticks suggest arguments and partings.

b) Leaves clustered around sticks bring bad news.

c) Dots or very small leaves suggest that the person repre-
    sented by the stick will bring the inquirer money.

d) A ring near a stick indicates a marriage.

Stocks

An embarrassing situation.

Stork

A baby coming, especially if this is near the handle.

Strawberries

Good times ahead, possibly a proposal of marriage. Finances will
improve.

Suitcase

Travel or visitors from over water.

Sun

This has a variety of meanings:

a) Happiness, success, influence, power.

b) A child could become important to the inquirer.

c) A new enterprise will flourish.

d) The summertime will be important and lucky.

e) A person born under the sign of Leo will be important.

f) If obscured, vanity and pride will bring a fall.

Sundial

Peaceful times ahead.

Swallow

a) A change for the better in every way.

b) Near the handle, protection to home and family.

c) A pleasant but unexpected journey to a hot place. If a business trip, success will follow.

Swan

A mixed bag of interpretations here:

a) Progress and a contented life.

b) An unexpected and unusual lover.

c) An improvement in finances.

d) At the bottom of the cup, death or separation from a long-term companion.

Sword

Quarrels, separations, divorce, loss, illness or even death around the inquirer. Crossed swords denote that strategic action will be needed, while a broken sword indicates defeat.

Table

a) A business conference or family council to be held.
b) Celebration; if near the handle, this will be in the home.
c) A nice new friendship.
d) If dots are nearby, a discussion about money.

Tambourine

Festivities and fun.

Telegram

Sudden news. Look for other omens, as this could be good or bad.

Telephone

An important call. Look for other omens, as this could be good or bad news.

Telescope

A mystery will soon clear up.

Tent

Travel or a period of restlessness. A need to get away for a while.

 Thimble

Domestic changes, perhaps a change of job. A fairly fortunate symbol.

 Thistle

A tough person who can survive anything or a time to be courageous.

 Thrush

An offer will be made.

 Tiger

Good luck in speculation.

 Toad

The inquirer should beware of flattery.

 Tongs

Restlessness and dissatisfaction, also sleepless nights.

Torch

Idealism and a desire for change. At the bottom of the cup or broken, a parting or a broken love affair.

Tortoise

Helpful criticism.

Tower

If the tower is in one piece, the inquirer is building something that will last. If incomplete, there will be a failure in plans.

Train

An unfortunate journey.

Tree

Recovery from illness, also ambition or wishes fulfilled.

Triangle

Unusual talent or creativity.

Trumpet

An announcement.

Trunk

A journey with a life-changing effect.

Tunnel

The inquirer will soon see his way clear.

Turkey

Celebrations and family get-togethers. If at the bottom of the cup, a collapse of plans.

Tusk

A lucky emblem and a better time for love and sex.

Umbrella

The inquirer will need help or even a roof over his head. If the umbrella is open, the inquirer will be given what she wants; if closed, she will not. If the umbrella is inside out, the inquirer will be responsible for her own difficulties or she may be in temporary difficulties. Disappointments.

Unicorn

A secret relationship or marriage.

Urn

Wealth and happiness. If near the rim, a birth; if near the bottom, a death.

Van

A move of house; note where the van is situated. A parcel arriving, business travel or making deliveries.

Vase

A friend will need help and advice. A time to make others happy.

Violet

One violet, modesty and sweetness; many violets, love and a happy home life.

Violin

A variety of meanings here:

    a) An increase in popularity but the inquirer should guard against this going to his head.

    b) Music and entertainment.

    c) An independent and very individual type of person will enter the inquirer's life.

Volcano

Passion and emotion or explosive burst of temper.

Vulture

Loss and theft, jealousy and spite.

Wagon

a) A wedding.
b) Breaking new ground and succeeding.
c) If the wagon is empty and near the bottom of the cup, the inquirer is better off shelving new plans for the time being.

Walking stick

A male visitor.

Wall

A time to build for the future but there will be obstacles to be overcome.

Wasp

Spiteful remarks, painful but perhaps justified criticism. Problems in love relationships.

Waterfall

Love, joy and enough money for comfort.

Weathercock

Indecision, possibly an unreliable lover.

Web

Intrigue, being caught up in a situation not of the inquirer's choosing. Also, she should not ignore sincere advice.

Wedding cake

A wedding.

Well

A wish will be granted.

Whale

Success in a large project that includes new ideas, or a maternal woman who is being taken advantage of.

Wheel

a) Progress and changes for the better. Earned success, rewards for past efforts.
b) Travel will be important.
c) If at the bottom of the cup, there will be a delay in proposed movements or impulsive action that could be harmful.

Wheelbarrow

Self-reliance and straightforwardness will be needed.

Whip

The inquirer should not be too domineering, but she will have the upper hand.

Windmill

A tricky venture that will work out well but that will require hard work. Even large schemes will be successful.

Window

The inquirer will have a clear vision of his future, and if the window is open, there will be new horizons. If closed or barred, obstacles and a lack of freedom. If dirty, the inquirer will not be as positive about his aims and aspirations.

Wineglass

Celebrations, overindulgence.

Wings

Messages from a distance or from over water. Look around for other symbols to tell whether these will be good or bad.

Wolf

a) Jealousy from surrounding people.
b) A swindle.
c) Can be a lucky sign if the inquirer has sick or teething infants.

Woman

Read this in combination with other symbols. If the woman is clear and uncluttered, there will be harmony and happy times, if clouded or surrounded by bad omens, jealousy or bad behavior from a woman. Also a desire for wealth and a happy family life.

Wreath

News of a death if near the bottom of the cup, otherwise a good sign.

Yacht

An easier lifestyle, possibly due to retirement. A good financial position.

Yew-tree

a) This can indicate a death or the loss of a partner or the ending of a relationship.
b) Achievements are possible in later life. The inquirer has not yet had the time to work towards these.
c) With dots nearby, a legacy.

Yoke

The inquirer should avoid being dominated by others.

Zebra

Either overseas adventures and a wandering lifestyle, or a love affair that will be enjoyable as long as it is kept secret.

About the Author

Sasha Fenton was born in Bushey, near Watford in Hertfordshire, England, and many members of her family have had an interest in psychic or occult subjects. Sasha became interested in palmistry in childhood, partly due to the fact that her mother knew something about it, although Sasha learned her craft initially from books and later by studying people's hands directly.

During her twenties, Sasha read and learned all she could about astrology, and by the time of her Saturn return, around the age of 30, Sasha was earning a little pocket money by preparing horoscopes for clients. She soon added Tarot reading to her list of skills, as well as Chinese divination methods. Sasha is a past Secretary and President of the British Astrological and Psychic Society (BAPS), a past Chairman of the British Advisory Panel on Astrological Education and a past member of the Executive Council of the Writers' Guild of Great Britain.

Sasha is the author of various books in the Orion Plain and Simple series, including: *Body Reading*, *Chakras*, *Palmistry* and *Sun Signs*.

Try another practical guide in the ORION PLAIN AND SIMPLE series